CHURCH
FOSTERING

Revitalization Through Strategic Partnership

RYAN K. COFFEY

ACKNOWLEDGEMENTS

First, I want to say thank you to my wife, Holly. Thank you for the many sacrifices you have made during this journey. You have prayed, supported, and encouraged me every step of the way. I could not have done this without you. I love you, Love.

To my children, Ty and Campbell. Thank you for the many sacrifices you have made as well. Your hugs, laughter, and encouragement sustained me during some of the most difficult days of life and ministry. I appreciate your kindness, support, and understanding through it all. Being your father is one of the greatest privileges of my life. Ty, seven rules. Campbell, always remember.

To my parents, Tom and Donna Coffey. Mom, thank you for your encouragement and example of being a devoted Christ-follower, caregiver, and author. Dad, thank you for teaching me the Gospel and showing me what matters most in life. I miss you every day.

To the congregations I have served in ministry. I hope I have ministered to you half as much as you have ministered to me. You have been a blessing to me and my family, and you have become some of the biggest cheerleaders in our lives. It was at your encouragement that I began this journey, by your prayers I was sustained, and with your support that I was able to see it through to completion. Thank you.

I am also grateful to the faculty and staff of NOBTS for their prayers, support, encouragement, and feedback throughout the process. I want to say a special thank you to Dr. Randy Stone, who served as my faculty mentor. Thank you to my field mentor, Dr. Rob Patterson, Kentucky Baptist Convention Evangelism Team Leader, and to all of those who were interviewed or contributed to the project in any way.

Finally, thank you to everyone who has encouraged, prayed for, and supported me during the process. The publishing of this handbook is one way for me to show my gratitude to the many people who supported and helped me reach this great milestone.

MULTIPY

SUPPORT

GO TO WORK

RELATIONSHIP

FOUNDATION

TABLE OF CONTENTS

INTRODUCTION

This Church Fostering Handbook was a part of my Final Project at New Orleans Baptist Theological Seminary (NOBTS) while completing my Doctor of Ministry. Pursuing and completing my DMin was a deeply rewarding experience that, in many ways, has prompted new seasons of personal and professional growth. It also fueled an already existing passion of mine related to church revitalization through strategic partnerships.

If you ask me what I am most passionate about in ministry, hands down, my first response will be church revitalization. It is evident that the church at large is struggling with countless local congregations closing their doors every year. While there has been much emphasis on church replants or adoption in recent years, creative solutions such as church fostering are needed to support struggling congregations. Often, ministry revitalization partnerships result in the dissolution of a local congregation. However, church fostering creates strategic partnerships for the sole purpose of restoring the church in need to full vitality and autonomy.

The goal of church fostering is to keep more sanctuary doors open and to focus on restoring existing churches rather than replacing them. Will you join me in promoting and participating in the church fostering movement? Let's rebuild together!

- Ryan K. Coffey

HOW TO USE THIS RESOURCE

This resource was created for the purpose of assisting churches in the work of church fostering. The goal is to inform, inspire, and equip healthy churches to take the next step in this exciting work. This handbook should be used as a companion guide for future church partnerships and aid in the work of church fostering.

Who's It For?

This handbook was written for leaders and members of healthy churches. Everyone is invited to read, pray, and evaluate their role within the church fostering ministry model. Every member is encouraged to participate in the work and is invited to read the handbook to learn more about the role they can play. Primarily, this resource was written for the staff and ministry leaders who will implement the fostering strategy.

What's In It?

In the pages ahead, you will find key terms, definitions, a biblical foundation, and the five unique phases of church fostering. The handbook will include the best practices of church fostering and recommendations for building ministry partnerships that will succeed. The handbook also includes key insights from revitalization leaders, recommendations from leading voices in the field, and specific encouragements based on church fostering research. Unless noted otherwise, all Scripture references are in the English Standard Version (ESV).

What to Know Before You Begin?

Church fostering is a multifaceted and often complicated ministry with a variety of circumstances that can dictate a church's response to a congregation in need. Each fostering relationship will be different and there is no one-size-fits-all approach. As lamented by Jay Strother, "you will quickly discover that church fostering is more of an art than a science."[1]

This means that the proposed church fostering strategy is meant to be fluid, with a high degree of flexibility in your church's response to every fostering relationship. Church fostering is designed to mirror the work of the familial foster care system in which loving guardians are entrusted with the care of a child and given the responsibility to provide structure, accountability, support, and stability. As each child within the foster care system has different needs, wants, and past experiences, so too will each unhealthy church prove to be different. These variances will require the healthy church to respond in general ways, while also recognizing the uniqueness of each church and the specific services that are needed.

Therefore, use this handbook as a guide and compass for the journey, but please allow the Holy Spirit to lead. Successful "church fostering requires pastoral intuition, flexibility, adaptability, and a keen sensitivity to the leading of the Holy Spirit."[2] Allowing the Holy Spirit to lead will remove the rigidity of policies and procedures and replace them with the rhythm and life of following Him. So, as you begin this journey, lean into the Word of God, follow the leading of the Holy Spirit, and trust God to bring revitalization through the fostering experience as He sees fit.

CHAPTER 1
PRELIMINARY QUESTIONS

A s you begin this journey, there are a few preliminary questions that must be addressed. This chapter will seek to answer the questions:

"What is church fostering?"

"Why is it needed?"

"What does the Bible say about it?"

"How can we help?"

As you read this chapter, I encourage you to take notes, pray, and form your own personal and biblical rationale for the ministry of church fostering.

What is Church Fostering?

According to the North American Mission Board, church fostering is defined as,

"Church foster care is a time-bound strategic partnership of a stronger church and a struggling church. Whereby the struggling church receives and accepts coaching, care, wisdom, and resources, aimed at returning the struggling church to vitality and full autonomy."[3]

The North American Mission Board's definition includes four significant terms of church fostering. These terms include *"time-bound," "stronger church," "struggling church,"* and *"return to vitality and full autonomy."* Let's take a closer look at these four components and how they inform the work.

Time-Bound:

Successful church fostering includes a specific time frame in which the proposed partnership will take place. Answers regarding the appropriate amount of time for a partnership will vary by preference, need, and location. Some leaders advocate for short partnerships, believing the work can be accomplished in a few months, while others prefer longer commitments lasting up to five years. Although answers vary by location and need, each leader interviewed for this project agreed, the time-bound element was a necessary component of the partnership.

Most experts interviewed for the project recommended a church fostering partnership that lasts between one and two years, with the goal being approximately eighteen months. This recommendation is based on the belief that less than one year would be an insufficient amount of time to address significant concerns, while relationships lasting beyond two years could create an unhealthy sense of dependency with the struggling church. Therefore, the goal for a healthy fostering relationship should be to establish a timeline lasting for a period of one to two years.

Stronger Church:

"Stronger Church" represents the church that is most spiritually healthy in the relationship and operates as a New Testament church. The title "stronger church" is not based upon attendance, budget, or overall size of the building or campus, but rather the church's health, ministry fruit, and commitment to following Scripture. In the fostering relationship, emphasis is placed on health over size.

To emphasize this point, the handbook will substitute the term "stronger church" for "healthy church" or "HC." If at any point the stronger church becomes spiritually unhealthy and declines rapidly, church leaders are encouraged to assume the role of the weaker church and seek outside help.

This handbook assumes the primary audience engaging with the text is from the healthy church or "stronger church." Churches in need may also find value in reading the work, but it may not address questions or concerns from that specific perspective.

Struggling Church:

"Struggling Church" is the name given to a church in need. The church in need will be referenced in the handbook as "CNF" (Church in Need of Fostering). A CNF represents any existing church that could benefit from partnering with a stronger, healthier, and missionally-focused congregation. In most cases, CNFs are lacking in several areas of measurable church health, which can include: the condition of their church property, polity and pastoral leadership, congregational vitality, and community involvement. The church fostering model seeks to bring revitalization and renewed health to these four areas through the process of strategic partnership with a healthy congregation.

Vitality and Full Autonomy:

Perhaps the most significant portion of the church fostering definition is found in the phrase, "aimed at returning the struggling church to vitality and full autonomy."[24] This portion of the definition sets church fostering apart from other similar and competing models of revitalization, such as adoption and replanting. Similar attempts to partner and revitalize declining churches often end with the healthy church taking over or replacing the weaker church with new leadership and members. In this case, the struggling church is often dissolved, or the building becomes a satellite campus of the stronger church. Although this model has been successful and needed in many locations, the hallmark commitment of church fostering is to see the struggling church revitalized and remain an autonomous local body of believers.

The goal of church fostering is to help the church in need reach a place where they are no longer dependent upon the outside help of others, but rather they are spiritually healthy and fully dependent upon God.

Why is it Needed?

The state of the American evangelical church is in decline. The exact number of churches closing annually remains unknown, but some estimates range between 3,500-7,500 each year.[5] As just one example, the Southern Baptist Convention (SBC) is currently closing nearly 1,000 churches annually.[6] To offset this historic rate of church closures, the Southern Baptist Convention and the North American Mission Board have proposed church planting as a leading strategy to fight this epidemic.

Church planting is the process of identifying unreached communities and starting new Gospel-proclaiming churches in those areas. The modern church planting movement has proven to be widely successful and has helped replace many closed churches. However, church planting does very little to prevent church closures and falls short of making up for the loss of Kingdom resources. Currently, Southern Baptists should be commended for planting between 300-400 churches a year, but at best, appear to be still falling short of replacing or breaking even with the 1,000 locations closed annually.[7] By solely focusing on church planting, the Southern Baptist Convention is left with a deficit of 600-700 churches annually and the stark reality that the global church is losing ground. Something else must be done.

Church fostering is one of the proposed strategies to tackle this epidemic. Successful church fostering is believed to be effective because it both prevents church closures and inspires new and additional works of revitalization moving forward. Revitalization through church fostering could be the missing piece that helps solve a very real and complex problem facing denominations like the Southern Baptist Convention and the nation today.

What Does the Bible Say About It?

As helpful and necessary as church fostering may seem, apart from a biblical mandate to join in the work, any effort would be of little or lasting significance. A healthy church's desire to bless and encourage other congregations must be grounded in the Gospel and the Word of God. Thankfully, Scripture has a lot to say about this ministry. Church fostering, revitalization, Gospel partnerships, and the commitment to invest in other believers are Biblical themes found in both the Old and New Testaments.

For example, consider the mentorship between the Apostle Paul and young Timothy. In this relationship, the Word of God provides an example of a minister investing and training another pastor to lead and serve well. Fostering churches are encouraged to lean on such examples and model godly leadership for the church in need. Likewise, the story of Nehemiah rebuilding the wall gives us an example of God's people rallying together to address a physical structure. The rebuilding of the physical wall was a tangible illustration of how God was rebuilding His people spiritually. Fostering churches are encouraged to communicate the principles and practices of Nehemiah as they begin the work of rebuilding and revitalizing a church in need.

Similarly, Paul commended the Ephesians for helping establish the Colossian church, and he honored the Corinthians for giving support to the work in Jerusalem. These examples serve as biblical evidence of one congregation supporting another for the sake of the

Gospel. Using these illustrations and others to establish a biblical rationale is not difficult, but it must be accomplished for both congregations to understand the work they have been called to do.

To be clear, the Bible does not explicitly state, "Thou shall foster churches." But to be fair, neither will you find a verse that says, "Go plant churches" or "have a business meeting." Rather, we find consistent examples in scripture of believers making new believers, leaders encouraging other leaders, and churches assisting other congregations. The spirit of the church fostering movement is rooted in the biblical text and is a modern expression of these ancient practices. We know that the Lord has called us to make disciples, minister with one another, and make a difference both near and far. Church fostering is yet another avenue through which we can accomplish this same, exciting work.

Scripture also teaches us the immense worth of the local church in the eyes of Jesus. In fact, Jesus so loved the church, He laid down His life for her. He loves His church so much that one day He is coming again to receive her. He cares for His church so deeply that He has entrusted faithful men and women to serve, nurture, and meet the needs of His church until He comes again.[8] These truths inspire us, challenge us, and serve as the biblical foundation that compels us to go, love, serve, provide, correct, and foster churches in need. The local church is in need of this work, and our Savior is deserving of our best effort.

How Can We Help?

After answering these preliminary questions, learning more about church fostering, and evaluating the biblical evidence, it is now time to act. Healthy churches play a significant role in the church fostering movement. It is the goal of this handbook to answer questions related to this revitalization strategy. Here, readers will discover best practices, key insights, and candid assessments of partnerships that will and will not work. Let's begin by considering the following initial steps.

Pray

Pray for God to intervene and help healthy churches connect, partner, and minister to churches in need. Pray that God will breathe new life into unhealthy churches and use local congregations to join in His work. Remember, revitalization comes from God and not us. Psalm 127:1 says, *"Unless the Lord builds the house, those who build it labor in vain."*[9] Interested supporters should consider praying daily for the Lord to bless those laboring in this field as He builds up His church.

Encourage

Encourage church leaders (from both the CNF and HC) to partner well and see the work through to completion. Church fostering is rewarding, but it can also be difficult and frustrating at times. Leaders will need encouragement to keep going when hurdles and obstacles appear. Philippians 1:6 says, *"And I am sure of this, that he who began a good work in you will bring it to completion..."* Commit to providing encouragement to church leaders until the process is complete.

Prepare to Go

For the church fostering model to be successful, volunteers will be needed. Church fostering requires faithful men and women (of all ages and abilities) to make themselves ready for service. Those willing to participate in revitalization efforts for a struggling church should share their interest with church leaders. Joshua 3:5 says, *"Consecrate yourselves, for tomorrow the Lord will do wonders among you."* Preparing to go is a key step in the launch of any strategic church fostering partnership. Those interested in serving must begin now by preparing themselves for the physical, spiritual, emotional, and financial commitment ahead.

Be Humble

Desiring revitalization for another church is a noble cause that is worthy of our pursuit; however, this work belongs to the Lord and not us. Yes, the Lord can use a healthy and willing congregation to be the catalyst for change, but ultimately, revitalization begins and ends with God. Therefore, celebrate Him, give Him the glory, and trust Him with the results.

Additionally, humility should be encouraged within all congregations by recalling times when churches were not at their best. Most likely, there was a time in every church's history when the Lord breathed new life and brought renewed seasons of growth and vitality. These remembrances should call us to rejoice in the Lord and not ourselves. No matter how far a church has come or how "successful" a church may seem, none of us have fully arrived. There is still room to grow and so much to learn.

In fact, helping churches in need with internal congregational strengths may inadvertently expose some of the weaknesses of a healthier church. So, let's remain humble and protect against developing a superhero complex. Christians are not called to be Superman, and no church is meant to be a cavalry that comes riding into town to save the day. Collectively, a single group of servants cannot fix everything that is broken, but they can point others to the God who can. So, let's be humble, prepare to go, encourage one another, and pray. Then perhaps the Lord will allow us to bless others as we have been so greatly blessed.

CHAPTER REVIEW

KEY TERMS

CHURCH FOSTERING: Church fostering partners a healthy church with a church in need for the purpose of revitalization. This partnership has a predetermined amount of time with the goal of returning the church in need to greater health, vitality, and autonomy.

TIME-BOUND: Church fostering relationships operate for a predetermined amount of time, ranging from one to three years in length.

STRONGER CHURCH: Stronger church represents the healthiest and most biblically sound church in the relationship. Within this handbook, the "stronger church" is referred to as the Healthy Church (HC).

STRUGGLING CHURCH: Struggling church represents any church in need of outside help to continue ministry and return to the God-honoring practices of a New Testament church. Within this handbook, the "struggling church" is referred to as the Church in Need of Fostering (CNF).

KEY TAKEAWAYS

INVEST: Church fostering is rooted in the biblical text. God's Word gives examples of Christians helping Christians, pastors investing in other leaders, and churches supporting Gospel work in other communities.

PARTNER: Church fostering is a revitalization effort through strategic partnerships that prevents church closures and engages declining churches before closure or replanting becomes necessary.

ENGAGE: When participating in church fostering, one should pray, encourage others, prepare to go, and act with humility.

REVITALIZE: The ultimate goal of church fostering is to restore the CNF to full vitality and autonomy.

KEY REFLECTIONS

Are you burdened by the declining state of evangelical churches? What role do you believe church fostering can play in alleviating that burden?

_____

_____

_____

_____

_____

_____

_____

_____

_____

_____

_____

_____

_____

_____

_____

_____

_____

_____

_____

KEY REFLECTIONS

Describe a time when someone helped you or you assisted a person in need. How were you blessed by that experience?

_____

_____

_____

_____

_____

_____

_____

_____

_____

_____

_____

_____

_____

_____

_____

_____

_____

_____

_____

_____

KEY REFLECTIONS

If someone asked you to define church fostering, how would
you define the ministry?

_____

_____

_____

_____

_____

_____

_____

_____

_____

_____

_____

_____

_____

_____

_____

_____

_____

_____

_____

_____

KEY NOTES

MULTIPY

SUPPORT

GO TO WORK

RELATIONSHIP

FOUNDATION

CHAPTER 2
PHASE I: LAY A STRONG FOUNDATION

The first step of church fostering includes laying a strong foundation within the congregation of the Healthy Church (HC). This phase includes beginning initial conversations with existing church leadership, casting vision for how the congregation can respond, formally adopting church fostering as part of mission mobilization strategies, evaluating strengths and weaknesses, establishing a Church Fostering Leadership Team (CFLT), and creating a church fostering residency program.

Practice 1 – BEGIN
Begin Initial Conversations with Existing Church Leadership

Before blessing and serving other churches, the leadership of the HC must understand that successful church fostering begins at home. Leaders of the HC must begin open and honest conversations about the role they can play in fostering another location. Key leaders from the HC, including the pastor, staff, deacons, and ministry leaders must discuss the work and the commitment required. Church fostering is a rewarding effort, but it can also be difficult and challenging. HC leaders must be honest about the challenges, time commitment, cost, and be realistic about the services they can and cannot provide. These in-house conversations are designed to help church leaders define what church fostering will look like moving forward. In short, this step requires church leaders to determine if and how they can move forward together by setting basic guidelines and finding mutual agreement to begin the work.

Practice 2 – CAST

Cast a Clear and Compelling Vision

Once a consensus has been reached, the pastor and key leaders should begin communicating their intentions to the congregation. The process of communicating the HC's role in future work is referred to as vision casting. Vision casting is a process where leaders identify, communicate, and help the congregation better understand their future together. The purpose of vision casting is to answer questions pertaining to the necessity of the work, provide a brief overview of how the church will support the effort, and describe how God will be glorified along the way. Lay leaders are encouraged to assist in this process, but ultimately, the role of vision casting belongs to the pastor.

Practice 3 - ADOPT

Adopt Church Fostering into the Church's Mission Mobilization Plan

As the pastor, staff, and key leaders communicate the HC's vision for church fostering, questions will naturally emerge from the congregation. Church leaders should take the necessary time to answer questions, address concerns, and reassure people of the importance of the work. As the congregation better understands the vision for church fostering, key leaders should aim to adopt a formal resolution stating church fostering as a key component of the church's mission mobilization strategy. The church's plan should be summarized in a written statement and formally adopted by the congregation in a regular church meeting or business session consistent with church polity.

By adopting church fostering as part of the church's mission mobilization strategy, church leadership will have the support necessary to move forward with a church in need. If the greater body of the HC fails to support the work and adopt the resolution, the project cannot continue. Church leadership should reevaluate their proposal and make necessary changes suitable to the church's response, or take more time to explain and gain feedback from the congregation before moving forward. Church fostering requires more than the efforts of one person and cannot be fulfilled by the desire of the pastor alone.

The congregation of the HC should formally adopt and support the work prior to beginning a fostering relationship.

Practice 4 - EVALUATE
Evaluate Strengths and Weaknesses

In addition to defining and adopting church fostering as part of a mission mobilization strategy, the HC should also take personal and corporate inventories that evaluate their strengths and weaknesses. For the HC to be of greatest benefit to others, they should first assess and evaluate their own health, ministry effectiveness, condition of property, and identify Biblical attributes and ministry qualities worth emulating. HCs must ask the questions: What attributes do we possess that are worth imitating by others? What do we do well that is worth coaching and modeling for others?

Answers to these questions may include vibrant worship, biblical fidelity, discipleship pathways, evangelism strategies, age-graded ministries, or improvements to the campus. Regardless of the areas identified, the HC must understand its own strengths and areas of expertise before attempting to model or coach a CNF.

Likewise, HC leaders should also consider areas of weakness or areas for improvement. If HCs are honest about their shortcomings and allow time for growth and development, they will be better prepared to help others in need. Taking time to look within and address in-house concerns allows HCs to approach a CNF with greater humility. The objective here is not for the HC to be perfect in all areas of ministry before helping others, but rather, to gain a greater sense of self-awareness before walking others through the process of personal and corporate growth. The words of Jesus serve as a strong reminder that we should not *"point out the speck in another's eye while ignoring the log in our own,"* (Matthew 7:3-5). Successful church fostering requires congregations that are willing to assess their own strengths and weaknesses, gain a higher sense of self-awareness, and minister with humility in their areas of expertise.

Practice 5 - CREATE

Create a Church Fostering Leadership Team

After identifying strengths and weaknesses, areas worth imitating, and a list of potential services that can be provided, it is now time to establish a Church Fostering Leadership Team (CFLT).

The CFLT serves as the representative between the HC and the CNF. The CFLT is responsible for leading the fostering effort and addressing issues as they emerge. The CFLT's size, skill set, and role will vary based on need and should be determined by the pastor and affirmed by the church.

As the HC moves forward into the work of church fostering, the pastor and staff must be protected from becoming the key points of contact or the ones solely responsible for helping the CNF. Church fostering is a team effort, and establishing the CFLT ensures that other well-trained, Gospel-minded people are involved in the process to help it succeed.

Although the CFLT exists in part to protect the pastor and key staff members from becoming the sole source of communication or decision-making, the pastor and staff should remain actively involved throughout the fostering process. It is recommended that the pastor serve as an ex-officio member of the CFLT and be given the freedom to appoint staff members and lay leaders to serve at his discretion. The pastor's leadership, influence, and shepherding qualities will be vital to the overall project, and his pastoral guidance should be considered heavily in all deliberations. The CFLT is encouraged to consult with and update the pastor regularly with any concerns, advancements, or delays in progress.

CFLT members are expected to attend regular meetings with the CNF, serve as liaisons between the two parties, provide ongoing support and accountability, and function as mediators when conflicts or concerns arise. The CFLT plays a significant role in the fostering process, and therefore, members selected should be capable, fit for the job, and understand the gravity of the work at hand.

Practice 6 - DEVELOP

Develop a Church Fostering Residency Program

Additionally, HC leaders can strengthen the foundation of their church fostering ministry by developing a church fostering residency program. By establishing a church fostering residency program, the HC will connect willing and emerging leaders with ministry opportunities in the field. The residency program should be designed to train, equip, and challenge leaders to participate in revitalization ministry and take the lead in fostered locations. In theory, the residency program addresses the long-term needs of having available leaders within the HC as well as ensuring success in the CNF after the relationship has ended.

As the HC is successful in fostering a CNF, the opportunity to partner and foster multiple locations at the same time will emerge quickly. In this case, the need for well-equipped, capable leaders will grow exponentially. The HC will find it advantageous to begin developing leaders from within who can be assigned to serve alongside CNFs as needed. To combat this long-term need for more leaders, the HC should consider creating a residency program that invites lay leaders and ministry students to be trained to meet the specific needs of fostered churches. This program should be designed to give candidates real-time leadership training and opportunities to serve. Without a leadership pipeline, both the HC and the CNFs will struggle to find adequate replacements for interim leadership or existing pastors who need additional support.

Both parties, the HC and the CNF, cannot wait until the end of the agreement to begin looking for long-term solutions for their leadership concerns. The practice of developing leaders should begin from the onset of the fostering relationship and be continued throughout the HC's commitment to care for and foster churches in need.

CHAPTER REVIEW

⌃⌃

KEY STEPS

BEGIN: The pastor and key leaders of the healthy church begin conversations about the need to foster other congregations.

CAST: The HC pastor and key leaders cast a clear and compelling vision of how they can support a church in need.

ADOPT: The HC formally adopts church fostering as a key component of their mission mobilization strategy.

EVALUATE: The HC evaluates their own strengths and weaknesses before attempting to foster another church.

CREATE: The healthy church creates a church fostering leadership team that will take the lead and protect the church and pastor in future fostering relationships.

DEVELOP: HCs should develop a church fostering residency program and leadership pipeline to train and equip future leaders to serve.

KEY REFLECTIONS

List the qualities and attributes of your church that you
perceive to be strengths and worthy of emulating for others.

_____

_____

_____

_____

_____

_____

_____

_____

_____

_____

_____

_____

_____

_____

_____

_____

_____

_____

_____

_____

KEY REFLECTIONS

List areas of concern or ministry practices that should be evaluated prior to the fostering experience.

_____

_____

_____

_____

_____

_____

_____

_____

_____

_____

_____

_____

_____

_____

_____

_____

_____

_____

_____

_____

KEY REFLECTIONS

Consider how you might be willing to serve in the fostering ministry. Which roles best suit your giftedness? Which roles should you avoid?

KEY NOTES

MULTIPY

SUPPORT

GO TO WORK

RELATIONSHIP

FOUNDATION

CHAPTER 3

PHASE II: BUILD THE RELATIONSHIP

After a strong church fostering foundation has been laid and the ministry model affirmed by the congregation of the HC, it is now time to begin seeking a church in need to help. At this point, HC leaders will find it advantageous to notify area churches, state and associational leaders, and potential ministry partners about their desire to foster. Fostering candidates may become available through conversations with state and local leaders, but most often emerge from existing relationships with the pastor, key leaders, or personal connections from within the healthy congregation. Mike Glenn, of the Engage Church Network, says:

> "...most of our fostering relationships came from people we already knew, these were churches we already had association with, and pastors that were aware of our work."[10]

In his comments, Dr. Glenn highlights how fostering partnerships are often developed from relationships within the HC rather than outside sources. Regardless of the origin of the relationship, establishing, defining, and signing a written covenant agreement make up the second phase of church fostering.

Practice 1 – ESTABLISH

Establish the Relationship

After identifying a potential ministry partner, it is now time to establish the fostering relationship. To be clear, there is no exact formula or cookie-cutter process for this step.[11] In some instances, establishing the relationship will happen quickly, while other relationships may take months or even years to develop through regular and ongoing personal meetings. The key to this phase is to be intentional, allow for time and space, and not rush the process. Successful fostering relationships cannot be forced and should move forward slowly as both parties become increasingly more comfortable with the partnership.

As the fostering relationship is being established, both churches should ask honest and relevant questions pertaining to the partnership. Questions should include: Are we aligned theologically? Can we work together to achieve a common goal? Is there mutual trust, respect, and a willingness to partner in the work? Is the Lord leading in this direction and bringing the relationship together? As both parties answer these questions and others, they need to be honest about the direction the relationship is headed and their ability to work together.

Jim Bo Stewart of the North American Mission Board states, "If the relationship is not a good fit, it is better to walk away and wait for the right ministry partner, than to walk this road and frustrate members of both churches."[12] Stewart goes on to say, "Understand what is at stake. If the fostering effort fails, the church in need may never be open to another revitalization effort of any kind, ever again. Meaning, if the fostering effort fails, it may guarantee the death and eventual closure of the church in need."[13] Stewart's comments serve as a warning of the potential consequences when HCs fail to slow down the process and ensure the relationship is a proper fit.

Likewise, taking time to find the right partner for the fostering effort will be beneficial to the HC as well. Failed or unhealthy partnerships can harm momentum and stifle future work. It is important for the leaders of the HC to proceed with caution and prayerfully discern which church is willing and ready to accept help and follow the Lord's leading in the revitalization process.

Establishing the relationship is about finding a suitable partner to work with. The relationship is established through personal conversations and a willingness to get to know the other church and its key leaders. Although a lot of attention is given to the value of honest dialogue in this portion of the process, partners must not overlook the value of listening. In many cases, churches in need have been wounded, they are grieving, and they have stories to tell. Listen to their stories to gain trust, but also listen to better understand the work that is needed and how to respond.

Practice 2 – DEFINE
Define the Relationship

As the relationship is being established, conversations about the partnership will naturally emerge. These conversations are opportunities to talk, dream, cast vision and prepare the church in need for a bright and healthier tomorrow. Mark Clifton, Replant Team Leader, North American Mission Board says, "These conversations should be 30,000 ft., 10,000 ft., 5,000 ft., and ground level discussions."[14]

As both parties are dreaming and discussing their futures together, they should also be actively defining the relationship. In part, defining the relationship comes as a response to a series of hypothetical questions about the future together. As a young couple naturally discusses their life and future together before committing to marriage, so too should the HC define their relationship and dream about what a partnership could look like with the CNF. It is also worth noting that establishing the relationship and defining the relationship are not merely sequential but also cyclical. Meaning, the more we define the relationship, the more the relationship is established; and conversely, the more the relationship is established, the more it will be defined. Mark Clifton says,

"Defining the relationship should include conversations about the history of the church in need, assessing problems and internal conflict, gauging how they view themselves, and understanding their active role in the community. As the conversation narrows in scope, expectations from both sides should be made clear. Negotiables and non-negotiables should be discussed with everyone, understanding the deal-breakers or what would end the fostering relationship.

Who will be in charge of money? Who will set the budget for next year? What about the teaching schedule or preaching rotation? Should the property and assets be relinquished to the healthy church? Is the church in need willing to suspend normal governance for six months or even a year until new systems and processes are put in place? All these questions and how they are answered ultimately define the relationship. If the conversation survives to this point, the relationship can move forward."[15]

Defining the relationship in this manner allows key leaders from both congregations to understand the direction the relationship is headed. As both parties find agreement on these questions, their conclusions and intentions should be communicated to the members of their respective churches. Clifton suggests, "the church in-need should give regular updates at business meetings, weekly gatherings and even special called town hall meetings as necessary."[16] The purpose of these meetings is to provide regular communication that protects both congregations from any potential surprises or misunderstandings pertaining to the fostering agreement.

Practice 3 - SIGN
Develop and Sign a Covenant Agreement

As the fostering relationship is established and defined, both parties should work together to develop and sign a written covenant agreement. Signing the covenant agreement is the climax of *Phase II*. The covenant agreement should contain at least two sections, which include, in detail, the intentions and responsibilities of both churches in the relationship. Church fostering is not a one-sided relationship or hostile takeover; it is a mutual agreement to grow and return the church in need to a renewed state of health. Therefore, the signed covenant agreement should contain multiple sections that use clear and decisive language to express the role and intentions of both churches. The church in need must clarify its willingness to accept help, suspend governance, and yield authority to the healthy church as agreed upon for a predetermined period.

The healthy church should outline its role, responsibility, and desire to return the church in need to a season of greater health, ministry effectiveness, and the pursuit of remaining a local, autonomous body of believers. The covenant agreement should also include the time-bound portion of the commitment by clearly identifying both the start and finish dates as agreed upon.

It is important to note, failure to sign a written covenant agreement should result in suspending or terminating the fostering relationship. If elements of the agreement can be amended appropriately for both parties, then take time to address the concerns and make the proper adjustments to secure the deal. However, certain non-negotiables (such as governance, time frame, financial commitment, property, etc.) cannot be compromised. If the struggling church is unwilling to sign a written covenant agreement, the HC must be prepared to walk away and find another partner to bless.

As the details of the covenant are agreed upon, leaders from both churches are encouraged to sign, date, and adopt the covenant agreement at a formal church gathering or special event. The signing and adoption of the covenant agreement should be celebrated by both churches to commemorate God's work and to rejoice in their newfound season of ministry together. The CNF should celebrate the signing of the document with hopeful anticipation of a new season in the church's history, and the HC should celebrate their willingness to bless others as the Lord has so blessed them.

Leaders from both churches should view the covenant agreement as a binding document. However, there may be cases where it is in the best interest of one or both churches to dissolve the agreement and go their separate ways. As such, the covenant agreement should outline the agreed-upon steps for dissolution. Additionally, both churches will discover that "church fostering is more of an art than a science."[17] Both churches will need to remain flexible, as some circumstances will dictate a response or decision that was not clearly stated in the agreement. When unforeseen issues arise, the CFLT and key leaders from both churches should commit to pray, seek wise counsel, employ pastoral intuition, be sensitive to the leading of the Holy Spirit, and choose a path that is in the best interest of both parties that upholds the spirit of their original agreement.

CHAPTER REVIEW

KEY STEPS

ESTABLISH: HCs establish a church fostering relationship through regular and ongoing conversations with a CNF.

DEFINE: Both parties work together to define the relationship by narrowing the scope of the conversation to include specific requirements and possible deal breakers.

SIGN: The HC and CNF develop and sign a written covenant agreement that clearly outlines roles, expectations, and the time-bound component of the relationship.

KEY REFLECTIONS

Make a list of struggling churches in your area that may be in need of outside assistance.

KEY REFLECTIONS

Do you believe leaders from those congregations would be willing to yield authority to another church until they returned to greater health?

_____

_____

_____

_____

_____

_____

_____

_____

_____

_____

_____

_____

_____

_____

_____

_____

_____

_____

KEY REFLECTIONS

List important details that you would want outlined in the signed covenant agreement.

_____

_____

_____

_____

_____

_____

_____

_____

_____

_____

_____

_____

_____

_____

_____

_____

_____

_____

_____

_____

KEY NOTES

MULTIPY

SUPPORT

GO TO WORK

RELATIONSHIP

FOUNDATION

CHAPTER 4

PHASE III: GO TO WORK

After developing and signing the covenant agreement, it is now time to go to work. This is the moment both churches have been waiting for. It is important to note that skipping ahead to *Phase III* without proper attention to *Phases I* and *II* could be catastrophic and undermine the completion of the work. Fady Al-Hagal says,

> "Do not let your compassion for the church in need or your desire to help shortcut the process. Building trust, establishing the relationship, and defining the terms of the agreement are necessary steps that cannot be overlooked."[18]

Once the HC has successfully moved through the first two phases, then, and only then, is it time to begin *Phase III*. This phase includes coaching, providing resources, and sending mission teams to address four specific areas for the CNF: the physical building, pastoral leadership, the spiritual health of the congregation, and how to reengage their community with the Gospel.[19]

Practice 1 – RESTORE

Restore the Property

One of the most advantageous strategies for a successful launch of the fostering relationship is prioritizing the physical needs of the building(s) and beautifying the campus. Addressing physical needs and restoring the building should give the fostering relationship an early and easy win. No, changing paint colors and decluttering Sunday school rooms does not bring revitalization, but the unified effort of both churches will represent the first of many future gains. As attention is given to the physical building, the HC can expect the CNF to experience renewed excitement and regain a healthy sense of pride and ownership of their building.

Efforts to address the physical campus should include deep cleaning, decluttering, and removing broken, outdated, and unused objects. The CFLT should mobilize teams to address external renovations such as curb appeal, refresh landscape, install new signage, and evaluate outdoor lighting. Inside the building, the children's area, nursery, youth space, Sunday school rooms, and sanctuary should be the highest priority.

The HC can provide volunteers to help with manual labor and offset some of the expenses as needed. As a co-laborer in the project, the HC may choose to financially bless the church in need with these projects. However, that should not excuse the CNF from fully paying for their own renovations to the extent they are capable. These expectations should also be outlined in the signed covenant agreement. Regardless of who funds the effort, both churches should participate in the physical labor and remember that the renewed building is meant to serve as a tangible preview of the restorative work God will do in the real church: His people.[20]

Practice 2 – REFRESH

Refresh the Pastor

Secondly, attention must be given to the pastoral leadership of the church in need. The HC should work to know, bless, and encourage the existing pastor of the CNF. In some cases, the existing pastor will be found in need of care, rest, resources, and encouragement before continuing the work. In this case, intentional efforts should be made and time allowed for the pastor to rediscover his God-given call, unique giftedness, and the role God has called him to play in the revitalization process.

In other cases, the pastoral leadership and church may come to realize the pastor is no longer suited for the role and his season of ministry is coming to an end. In this case, the HC should allow time for the Holy Spirit to lead the pastor's steps rather than dictating those moves for him. As the fostering church, the HC's role is to bless, encourage, and ensure the right man for the job is leading the CNF moving forward. In cases where a pastor is already in place, the HC should evaluate the pastor's needs and formulate a plan to respond.

In some scenarios, the church in need will be without a pastor, and the HC should assist the CNF in the pastor search process. Assisting with this work may include locating a suitable interim, helping to establish a pastor search team, collecting resumes, or even recommending candidates for the job. The HC can also provide interim leadership or pastoral teams to assist the CNF until a permanent or suitable candidate is found.

Additionally, the HC may discover the church in need has other concerns related to leadership, governance, and decision-making. These concerns will be addressed later in *Phase IV: The Work Continues*. However, it should be noted that the existing leadership and the leadership structure should be evaluated, discussed, and addressed throughout the entirety of the process. Addressing these concerns up front, modeling biblical church polity, and spurring the CNF to greater health will require ongoing discussions about healthy church leadership. From this perspective, refreshing leadership goes far beyond addressing the role of the pastor and moves into a greater discussion of polity and God-honoring decision-making practices. However, for this phase, the primary step is to specifically address the health of the pastor and ensure a God-honoring leader is in place.

Practice 3 - REFOCUS

Refocus the People

The third component of *Phase III* is addressing the spiritual condition of the congregation. Perhaps the most difficult part of church fostering is helping the CNF to see their unhealthy condition as a spiritual concern rather than a problem related to a lack of infrastructure. Too often, struggling churches believe that the decline of people and resources is their greatest problem while ignoring the symptoms of a slow and gradual spiritual decline. To address this concern, the pastor and CFLT are encouraged to conduct a congregational health assessment. This evaluation should include a thorough review of the CNF's past Annual Church Profile, church trend profile, and demographic study that compares the church with its community. This data can be made available through church records and with the assistance of denominational leaders.

These resources can help the declining church better recognize losses and unhealthy trends from an objective source. Following downward trends of the church, perhaps over many years, can help the CNF work through preconceived notions, eliminate long-held excuses, and reduce the finger-pointing that often blames a single person or problem for their condition. In many cases, declining churches will discover a slow fade, over time, that occurred across the leadership of multiple pastors.

Through this investigative process, the declining church may also discover a disconnect from its community. In many cases, churches fail to meet the needs of a changing community around them. In such cases, there is no one person or problem to blame, but rather a congregation unwilling to honor and follow the Lord's mission for His church.[21]

Reviewing church records, establishing trends, and conducting demographic studies may expose significant weaknesses and prompt a sense of urgency within members of the CNF. It is at this point, the HC and the CFLT play a major role in helping the church in need regain an appropriate sense of urgency. Mark Clifton states,

> "Struggling churches have a sense of urgency, but it's misplaced urgency. They are thinking about infrastructure. How can we get more people and more money to keep doing what we've been doing and stay alive longer? A right sense of urgency is the urgency to honor and serve the Lord. To bring Him glory in all we do."[22]

Clifton's evaluation of the need for an appropriate sense of urgency is a significant part of this practice. For many churches in need, the desperation to survive and continue as-is has replaced the godly ambition to please the Lord and follow His commands. The remedy for this condition can only be found in a return to God's Word and the practices that bring Him glory. The HC's primary role in this step is to refocus the congregation's attention on the Gospel and God's calling for His church.

Addressing the spiritual health and the decline of the congregation includes a call to repentance, a change of heart, and the Holy Spirit exposing the discrepancies between daily practices and the truth of God's Word. Due to the sensitive nature of this portion of the work, a shepherd is required and not a strategist![23] By God's design, He will work in the spiritual lives of His people through the teaching, leadership, and gentle correction of a godly shepherd. Other areas of church fostering allow for teams of specialists to provide pragmatic solutions; however, this area belongs to those with shepherding gifts and pastoral experience. Refocusing the congregation and revitalizing their spiritual health should be the joint effort of both churches, but must be primarily led by the pastor and CFLT of the HC.

Practice 4 – REENGAGE

Reengage the Parish

The fourth and final component of this phase involves giving attention to the ministries and missional mindset of the congregation. In the words of Mike Glenn, "Church fostering is Missionary 101. Help them understand the culture, context, and language. Know the community in which you exist and then figure out how to reach that community. If I dropped you off in Japan, you would learn Japanese. They need to relearn the language of their community."[24]

Glenn's assessment of the need to reclaim a missional mindset perfectly captures the work and sentiment of this fourth practice. The role of the HC is to help the CNF view their local community as a mission field and then help them create outreach strategies to reach those near the church. The goal of this step is to move the fostered church beyond the four walls of its own building and increase its Gospel impact in the local community.

Developing a missional mindset and convincing the CNF to adjust existing ministries to become more outwardly focused rather than inwardly focused will take time. There are many ways to approach this portion of the work, but beginning with a demographic study and assessing the needs of the community is a great place to start. Fady Al-Hagal, Multiplication Pastor, Brentwood Baptist Church, Brentwood, TN, says:

"This has become my starting place. If we start with evaluating the church and pointing out everything that is wrong, they get defensive. It stirs up emotions of grief, past hurts, and trauma. When we start by assessing them, we unintentionally create hurdles and roadblocks that we will have to work through later. Therefore, we start with assessing the community. Who lives around you? What are their needs? How can we meet those needs?"[25]

Helping the church in need better understand their community and assisting them in strategic outreach opportunities is an important part of this phase. This work can include canvassing the community with a survey, distributing food or gifts, hosting a block party or community event, and sponsoring a local school. There are many ways to serve the community and increase community awareness of the local church. Regardless of how the church chooses to invest and reengage in their own community, the main goal of these efforts is to help the CNF become reacquainted with those living closest to them. Church leaders are encouraged to identify needs in their own community and prayerfully consider the condition of lostness, brokenness, and unmet physical needs.

Mike Glenn states, "These are three areas the church, historically, has been successful in working. Many of our colleges and universities were founded by church leaders, same is true for our hospitals and healthcare system and no one has helped meet the needs of the poor like Christians have. Our job is to help them meet needs in these three areas in their own backyard."[26]

Helping the CNF address education, health care, and poverty-related needs, as well as the spiritual condition of their community, moves them one step closer to becoming missionally minded. The HC's role is to help identify these potential areas of service and to create strategic outreach opportunities that mobilize the CNF into their own community. Additional help in this area can also include teaching the CNF how to reallocate funds, train volunteers, and encourage ministry leaders to remain focused on the community rather than accommodating the preferences of church members.

Phase III: Go to Work is the centerpiece of all church fostering strategic partnerships. This is where real-life change, revitalization, and new growth occur. This is also where relationships get messy, the work gets tough, and prayer and encouragement are a priority. At this stage of the process, each fostered church will require a different level of work, varying degrees of added attention, and an abundance of patience. HCs should use this chapter as a template for beginning the work and as a source of encouragement to address needs pertaining to the property, pastor, people, and parish.[27]

CHAPTER REVIEW

KEY STEPS

RESTORE: The CFLT encourages, supports, and enables the CNF to prioritize physical improvements to the church campus and building(s) as an advantageous first action step in the strategic partnership. The visible evidence of a revitalized building can foreshadow the spiritual work God will do in His people. (Property)

REFRESH: HCs assist with evaluation of the overall health of the existing pastor and, if necessary, provide respite, interim leadership, and/or new leadership search. This practice calls for the healthy church to make sure the right man is leading for the next season of health and growth in the fostered church. (Pastor)

REFOCUS: Both parties begin the work of addressing the spiritual condition of the congregation. This work can be accomplished through strategic discipleship and a plan to help the CNF regain an appropriate sense of urgency. (People)

REENGAGE: The CFLT helps the church in need to reengage with their community through outreach events and evangelism strategies. The CNF should view their community as their primary mission field and then commit to reengaging those closest to their church. (Parish)

KEY REFLECTIONS

Of the four areas of ministry concern (Property, Pastor, People, or Parish), which component of the work are you most excited to assist with? Why?

_____

_____

_____

_____

_____

_____

_____

_____

_____

_____

_____

_____

_____

_____

_____

_____

_____

_____

_____

_____

KEY REFLECTIONS

Of the four areas of ministry concern (Property, Pastor, People, or Parish), which one do you feel most disconnected from? Why?

KEY REFLECTIONS

List three ways you can help a church in need reengage
their community with the Gospel.

_____

_____

_____

_____

_____

_____

_____

_____

_____

_____

_____

_____

_____

_____

_____

_____

_____

_____

_____

KEY NOTES

MULTIPY

SUPPORT

GO TO WORK

RELATIONSHIP

FOUNDATION

CHAPTER 5
PHASE IV: PROVIDE ONGOING SUPPORT

As the church fostering relationship moves forward, the HC must be intentional about creating both short-term and long-term success. Beginning with addressing the physical campus allows the partnership to have an immediate, short-term win, but what about long-term success? Can the spiritual renewal and revitalization of God's people be sustained for a prolonged period? Who will be responsible for ensuring outreach strategies or newly installed evangelism practices will be maintained after the partnership has ended?

The purpose of this chapter is to outline the additional and ongoing support necessary for the fostering relationship to succeed long-term. The strategy, as presented up to this point, is thought to be effective and all-encompassing in many ways. However, several areas of ongoing support must be provided to ensure sustained success. These areas include leadership development and ministry training, addressing church polity and poor decision-making practices, providing regular and ongoing communication, and making the commitment to share the story of how God is working in the fostering relationship.

Practice 1 – TRAIN

Ministry Training and Leadership Development

The first area of ongoing and long-term support for CNFs can be provided through leadership development and ministry training events. Leaders from the HC should create a series of ministry training events and service opportunities to better equip the fostered church to thrive after the partnership has ended. The HC can meet this need by hosting a one-day ministry training event, a weekend retreat, or providing a series of meetings for leaders from the church in need.

Ministry training events should be designed to reinforce the missional mindset and to better equip volunteers on how to identify and capitalize on ministry opportunities within their own community. Ministry training should also include how to share the Gospel, how to connect with new families, how to follow up after ministry events, and how to assimilate new people into the congregation. Details of these ministry trainings will vary by location, need, and availability of key leaders. Regardless of how the trainings are offered, the HC should commit to training and equipping ministry leaders to serve. Once again, the purpose of these ministry training events is to help leaders and volunteers from the CNF take the lead in ministry and thrive once the proposed time frame has ended.

As stated in *Phase I: Lay a Strong Foundation*, the HC is encouraged to create a church fostering residency program and leadership pipeline. This pipeline should be established to meet long-term leadership needs in both the HC and the CNF. As the HC actively pursues fostering relationships, the need for well-equipped, capable leaders will only grow. The HC will find it advantageous to begin developing leaders from within and seeking others from without who are willing to grow, learn, and serve CNFs as needed. Without a residency program or leadership pipeline, both HCs and CNFs will struggle to find adequate replacements for interim leadership or existing leaders in need of transition. The pastors from both churches, the CFLT, and key leaders should partner together to identify, equip, and help new leaders thrive in revitalization settings.

It is important for both parties that the HC and the CNF do not wait until the end of the agreement to begin looking for long-term solutions to their leadership needs. The practice of developing leaders should remain part of the HC's long-term commitment to this ministry. When proactive leadership development is embedded into the church fostering ministry, both HCs and CNFs will feel well-served, supported, and blessed. Ministry training and leadership development listed here, in *Phase IV,* is meant to underscore the value of good leaders and the short supply of their existence. Whether future leaders come from the HC, the CNF, or outside sources, training and equipping them well is key to the church fostering model.

Practice 2 – CORRECT

Correcting Church Polity and Decision-Making Practices

In addition to the HC's commitment to leadership development and ministry training, the need to address church polity and poor decision-making structures of the CNF will be needed. CNFs often operate with antiquated decision-making practices, a poor leadership structure, or governing documents that limit ministry practices. The HC should help the CNF revisit, correct, and properly align the church's polity to reflect a biblical and God-honoring structure.

In this portion of the ongoing work, the CNF pastor and the CFLT should carefully evaluate the church's leadership, decision-making process, constitution, and bylaws, as well as search for weaknesses within their regular business practices. For what would the CNF gain if they experienced revitalization, then quickly returned to an ineffective leadership structure that undermined the work when the partnership was over? To protect against this type of long-term failure, the CFLT will be tasked with evaluating the roles of the pastor, deacons, and other leaders within the church. The HC should not be surprised to uncover governing deacon bodies, ruling patriarchs or matriarchs within the church, or a vocal minority that limits ministry effectiveness. In such cases, HC leadership and the CFLT should lovingly instruct, guide, and appropriately deal with these roadblocks to greater church health.

Additionally, the frequency of business meetings and business practices will be under heavy scrutiny, along with the content, motions, and recorded discussions from those meetings. The HC should work to liberate the CNF from any self-destructive practices that limit ministry effectiveness. These practices may include micromanaging finances, requiring unnecessary steps of approval, or not allowing the pastor and staff to lead properly. The HC should also help the CNF with business-related tasks such as developing an annual budget, proper record-keeping, and producing transparent financial statements for the congregation. As weaknesses are identified, the HC should work to educate, model, and streamline the decision-making process for the CNF in a manner that protects the church and honors the Lord. The two-fold purpose of this step is to eliminate organizational dysfunction while simultaneously restructuring church polity to support long-term health.

Practice 3 - COMMIT

Commit to Regular and Ongoing Communication

As part of the ongoing support and commitment to the CNF, the CFLT should plan to meet regularly with key leaders from both churches. These meetings should be scheduled in advance, and the commitment to participate in these necessary discussions should be agreed upon in the signed covenant agreement. Church leaders from both locations should expect to meet at least monthly during the first year and more often as needed during strategic times. As these regular meetings unfold, leaders from both churches are expected to attend, listen, learn, and encourage one another in the process.

Meetings between the two churches should take place on both campuses as a sign of their commitment to one another and as part of the ongoing practice of building trust, familiarity, and a desire to learn from each other. The CNF can be inspired by these off-campus meetings to pursue new heights of ministry growth and congregational health. Allowing time for CNF leaders to tour facilities and have access to HC resources can help them gain a new perspective and envision a revitalized church. Meanwhile, the HC can be encouraged and challenged by visiting the CNF. On-site visits made by HC leaders can help them recapture the relational intimacy of a smaller congregation and remember the contagious energy of rebirth. Regular meetings among pastors, staff, deacons, ministry leaders, volunteers, and the CFLT are an important part of the ongoing commitment to one another.

Additionally, regular meetings help keep the lines of communication open throughout the duration of the fostering relationship. Inevitably, conflict, misunderstandings, and obstacles will emerge through the fostering process. Regular and ongoing meetings allow the appropriate time and space for concerns to be aired, dealt with, and reconciled without prolonging the conflict or allowing hurt feelings to remain unaddressed. Consistent gatherings and ongoing communication must be scheduled and practiced by both parties in the relationship.

Regular meetings serve as the primary source of accountability for the relationship. During the meetings, members of the CFLT are encouraged to document needs, concerns, and propel the fostering effort forward with regular updates. These updates include a review of previous discussions, a record of ongoing conversations, and a strategy for work that needs to be accomplished prior to the next meeting. In short, regular and ongoing communication provides accountability, promotes transparency, and strengthens the relationship in many ways. Without these regular meetings, the work could stall, and the relationship could break down. A commitment to gather, pray, and co-labor regularly remains a best practice of successful fostering relationships.

Practice 4 – SHARE

Tell the Story

Finally, the ongoing support of church fostering includes telling the stories of what God is accomplishing through the fostering relationship. Ultimately, revitalization and church fostering are for God's glory, and His work should be commemorated. In many ways, the Lord can rewrite the story of both churches through the fostering relationship, and leaders should share this narrative before their respective congregations. This part of the ongoing commitment includes listening for, capturing, and retelling the story of God's work. As wins accumulate and gains are made, the HC should take the lead in sharing these stories with both congregations. Recording testimonies, allowing time for feedback at regular meetings, creating a video montage of special events, and hearing from key leaders along the way will help affirm, to both groups, the work God is doing.

These stories must be told by the pastors from both churches, but in many cases, they may be best delivered by the faithful saints who are in awe of God's redemptive plan. For example, churches should consider interviewing a long-time deacon who had once given up hope, a nursery worker who has more children to care for, or a new family that is serving and joining in God's restorative work. Recording testimonies and sharing these wins can also include the celebration of an increase in giving, worship attendance, baptisms, or the start of new outreach events. Wherever there is a win, celebrate it. Share the story of what God has done and is doing through the fostering relationship.

CHAPTER REVIEW

KEY STEPS

TRAIN: HCs provide ministry training events for volunteers and leaders of the CNF. Church members will need opportunities to learn new skills and participate in ministry training.

CORRECT: The CFLT will assist the CNF with evaluation of church polity and decision-making practices. Look for areas to streamline, and if necessary, correct the decision-making process to rightly align the church's governance in a biblical and God-honoring fashion.

COMMIT: Both parties must commit to regular and ongoing meetings. These meetings keep the lines of communication open, keep progress moving, and demonstrate a commitment to one another.

SHARE: Both parties agree to prioritize intentionally sharing all God is doing in the fostering relationship. Listen for, capture, and share stories of God's provision and allow individuals the opportunity to testify to God's work in their lives and in the church.

KEY REFLECTIONS

How can biblical church polity and healthy decision-making practices promote church health? How can unhealthy practices lead to a church's decline?

_____

_____

_____

_____

_____

_____

_____

_____

_____

_____

_____

_____

_____

_____

_____

_____

_____

KEY REFLECTIONS

The purpose of regular and ongoing communication is to promote transparency and accountability. If you were involved in monthly meetings with a church in need, what questions would you ask?

_____

_____

_____

_____

_____

_____

_____

_____

_____

_____

_____

_____

_____

_____

_____

_____

_____

_____

_____

KEY REFLECTIONS

Record a time when God used someone else's testimony to minister to you.

_____

_____

_____

_____

_____

_____

_____

_____

_____

_____

_____

_____

_____

_____

_____

_____

_____

_____

_____

KEY NOTES

MULTIPY

SUPPORT

GO TO WORK

RELATIONSHIP

FOUNDATION

CHAPTER 6
PHASE V: FINISH WELL

The fifth and final phase of church fostering is found in the commitment to finish well. As the agreed-upon relationship comes to an end, a few steps are necessary to ensure that both parties receive proper closure related to their labors and partnership together. To assist with this practice, the fostering relationship should not end until the CFLT has been able to properly evaluate the relationship, celebrate the completion of the work, and commission the restored church to invest in similar projects in the year to come.

Practice 1 – EVALUATE
Conduct Exit Interviews to Identify Key Takeaways and Provide Closure

The first step in finishing well is to implement a strong and deliberate evaluation system to interview key leaders, review the work, and spotlight the highs and lows of the fostering experience.[28] Each member of the CFLT should participate in an exit interview detailing their experience in the process. This interview should allow members of the team to express what they have learned, areas of concern, and tips on how to improve future fostering relationships. The pastor, church staff, and key leaders should conduct these interviews and create a ministry grid that allows them to track and record recommendations for future fostering relationships. Comments and recommendations from the ministry grid should be compiled into a best practice report that allows the church to have a record of recommended practices for future ministry partnerships. These recommendations should be kept by ministry leaders and even formally adopted by the church as part of their own church fostering resources.

The most crucial element of this step is to ensure that key leaders have an outlet to express their own concerns and be given an opportunity to record testimonies of their own experience. Leaders should be encouraged to evaluate the relationship, ministry practices, and expose both strengths and weaknesses from their perspective. Both churches should expect to learn from the fostering experience, and key lessons and takeaways should not be lost before moving on to another project. Taking time to debrief and evaluate the process will also provide an avenue of closure for those who have served closest to the project.

Practice 2 – CELEBRATE

Celebrate Strategic Partnership Completion

The second practice within this phase is choosing to celebrate the completion of the agreement. According to Mike Glenn, "This should be the biggest party in town. Rejoice together, honor key leaders, highlight memorable moments, worship the Lord for His faithfulness, and enjoy a celebratory meal."[29] The celebration can take place over a weekend, as a special event, or through a combined worship service on a Sunday morning.

This celebration is an opportunity to reflect on the work, rejoice in the Lord, and spotlight the key leaders who led throughout the relationship.

In addition to the initial celebration, plans can also be made for a one-year follow-up, or an invitation can be extended to the restored church to share their ongoing progress at other strategic times. Options for commemorating the project's completion are endless and will vary by location and context. Regardless of how the HC and the CNF choose to mark this milestone, a commitment to celebrate must be made. As the signing of the covenant agreement marks the official start of the relationship, the ending celebration serves as the ceremonial end. Both steps are necessary and provide clear start and end dates for the relationship.

Practice 3 - MULTIPLY

Commission the CNF to Go Out and Bless Others

After evaluating and celebrating the fostering relationship, the third and final component is to commission the fostered church to replicate the effort in another location. Commissioning the fostered church to bless or support other Gospel works should be included in the end celebration and followed up appropriately. Commissioning the CNF to support other works can include planting a new church, replanting an old one, sending mission teams to a church in need, or even co-fostering another location with the HC. By building multiplication into the process, additional layers of accountability are added to the work.

Commissioning the CNF to bless others guarantees, in part, that the revived church will continue to be missionally-minded rather than internally focused. Leaders from the HC should communicate this expectation to the CNF from the very beginning, as a source of encouragement and as an obtainable goal that they are fully able to reach. The commitment to multiply should be clearly stated in the signed covenant agreement, and both parties should be working toward this end throughout the partnership. Commissioning the CNF to other locations encourages a co-laboring model that can create a church fostering movement that is both cyclical and scalable.

Remember, the goal of church fostering is to help the CNF return to a greater level of health and vitality, remain an autonomous local church, and thrive once the partnership has ended. The challenge to multiply and replicate the work in other locations undergirds this goal and challenges the CNF to strive toward a greater work. The commissioning of the CNF is the culminating event of the fostering experience and should be celebrated as a crowning achievement.

CHAPTER REVIEW

KEY STEPS

EVALUATE: Both parties should participate in exit interviews and extensively document feedback about the fostering relationship. The church fostering leadership team and key leaders should be given the opportunity to debrief, evaluate their experiences, and make recommendations for future partnerships.

CELEBRATE: Both the HC and CNF should commit to celebrating the completion of the fostering relationship. The ending celebration provides closure to both parties and allows them to move on in an appropriate manner. This step is a key component of the church fostering ministry, should be agreed upon at the start of the strategic partnership, and included in the covenant agreement.

MULTIPLY: The strategic partnership should build multiplication into the process of church fostering. The revived church should be commissioned to go and partner with other churches in need or begin new Kingdom work in other locations. The effort to multiply creates a fostering movement that is cyclical and scalable.

KEY REFLECTIONS

Describe the importance of finding closure in ministry and choosing to finish well.

_____

_____

_____

_____

_____

_____

_____

_____

_____

_____

_____

_____

_____

_____

_____

_____

_____

_____

_____

KEY REFLECTIONS

Brainstorm ideas on how best to celebrate the conclusion of the fostering relationship.

_____

_____

_____

_____

_____

_____

_____

_____

_____

_____

_____

_____

_____

_____

_____

_____

_____

_____

_____

KEY REFLECTIONS

How can we build multiplication into existing ministries now?
How would you commission the fostered church to go and
do likewise?

_____

_____

_____

_____

_____

_____

_____

_____

_____

_____

_____

_____

_____

_____

_____

_____

_____

_____

KEY NOTES

MULTIPY

SUPPORT

GO TO WORK

RELATIONSHIP

FOUNDATION

CONCLUSION
FINAL WORDS OF ENCOURAGEMENT

Thank you for reading the church fostering handbook. I hope you have learned about the ministry, better understand the phases, and are ready to implement the practices. I believe the time has come for stronger churches to invest in struggling churches. Before moving forward, consider the following reminders and encouragements about the work.

As we embark on this church fostering journey, we must choose to act. The need for healthy churches investing in churches in need is perhaps greater now than ever before. The Lord has greatly blessed many churches with an abundance of resources, influence, and gifted people who can make a real and lasting difference in the Kingdom of God. There are many ways for healthy churches to impact the world, but perhaps none is more fitting for some than to invest in other congregations. If we hope to prevent church closures and aim to slow down the rate of church decline, we must choose to join in the fight. Let us:

- Lay a strong foundation.
- Build meaningful relationships.
- Go to work.

- Provide ongoing support.
- Choose to finish well.

May God continue to bless willing congregations that participate in His restorative work through the efforts of church fostering.

REMEMBER

Church fostering ...

1. **DOES** require the leading of the Holy Spirit, **SO** be discerning.

2. **IS** more of an art than a science, **SO** be flexible.

3. **DOES** take time to develop, **SO** be patient.

4. **IS** worth doing well, **SO** commit to excellence.

5. **DOES** demand that change must occur, **SO** stand firm.

6. **IS** built on trust, **SO** keep your word.

7. **DOES** expose problems, **SO** provide solutions.

8. **IS** not easy, **SO** persevere.

9. **DOES** invite others to co-labor, **SO** partner well.

10. **IS** always worth it, **SO** let's begin!

APPENDIX A

Sample Covenant Agreement

Church Fostering Covenant Agreement

Healthy Church, City, State and In-Need Church, City, State.
Month, 20xx – Month, 20xx

Article I

Covenant Agreement: Outline the general details of the relationship, the need, goals, and willingness to partner together.

Article II

Terms of Provision: Outline the roles and responsibilities of both churches.

Fostering church (HC) provides....
a. Funding for outreach events.
b. Leadership training.
c. Ministry teams to address four areas of concern.
Fostered church (CNF) commits to...

x. Funding projects to the fullest of their ability.

y. Yield authority for a set period.

z. Accepting the necessary changes for revitalization.

Together we will...

l. Commit to praying for revitalization.

m. Co-labor to address the physical needs of the campus.

n. Support the right pastor to lead the work.

o. Seek God's will for the church.

p. Engage the community for the sake of the Gospel.

Article III

Terms of Cancellation: Reaffirm the commitment to co-labor in the project but also include plans for dissolving the relationship if necessary.

Article IV

Terms of Celebration: Clearly identify the expected end date for the fostering relationship and how both churches intend to celebrate upon completion of the project.

Church Name	Signature	Date
_____	_____	___/___/___
_____	_____	___/___/___

APPENDIX B

Summary of Best Practices of Church Fostering

Phase I: Lay The Foundation

Practice 1: The pastor and key leaders of a healthy church begin the conversation about the need for fostering other congregations.

Practice 2: The pastor and key leaders cast a compelling vision of how the healthy church can support a church in need.

Practice 3: The healthy church formally adopts church fostering as a key component of their mission mobilization strategy.

Practice 4: The healthy church evaluates their own strengths and weaknesses before attempting to foster another location.

Practice 5: The healthy church creates a church fostering leadership team that will take the lead and protect the pastor in future fostering relationships.

Practice 6: Develop a church fostering residency program and leadership pipeline to train and equip future leaders to serve.

Phase II: Build the Relationship

Practice 1: Establish a church fostering relationship through regular and ongoing conversations with a church in need.

Practice 2: Define the relationship by narrowing the scope of the conversation to include specific requirements and possible deal breakers.

Practice 3: Sign a written covenant agreement that clearly outlines roles, expectations, and the time-bound component of the relationship.

Phase III: Go to Work

Practice 1: Give attention to the physical campus and make improvements to the church building. The visible evidence of a revitalized building can foreshadow the spiritual work God will do in His people. (Property)

Practice 2: Evaluate the existing pastor or provide an interim or preaching team to lead. This practice calls for the healthy church to make sure the right man is leading for the next season of health and growth in the fostered church. (Pastor)

Practice 3: Begin the work of addressing the spiritual condition of the congregation. This work can be done through a strategic discipleship plan and by helping them regain an appropriate sense of urgency. (People)

Practice 4: Help the church in need reengage their community through outreach events and evangelism strategies. The unhealthy church should view their community as their mission field and commit to reengaging those closest to them in proximity. (Parish)

Phase IV: Provide Ongoing Support

Practice 1: Provide ministry training events for volunteers and leaders of the church in need. Church members will need opportunities to learn new skills and ministry training.

Practice 2: Evaluate church polity and decision-making practices. Look for areas to streamline the decision-making process and rightly align the church's governance in a biblical and God-honoring fashion.

Practice 3: Commit to regular and ongoing meetings with leaders from the church in need. These meetings keep the lines of communication open, progress moving, and demonstrate the commitment to one another.

Practice 4: Be intentional about telling the story of what God is doing in the fostering relationship. Listen for, capture, and retell stories of God's provision and allow individuals the opportunity to testify to God's work in their life and in the church.

Phase V: Finish Well

Practice 1: Conduct exit interviews and keep extensive notes about the fostering relationship. The church fostering leadership team and key leaders should be given the opportunity to debrief their experience and make recommendations for future partnerships.

Practice 2: Commit to celebrating the completion of the fostering relationship. The ending celebration provides closure to both parties and allows them to move on in an appropriate manner.

Practice 3: Build multiplication into the process of church fostering. The revived church should be commissioned to go and partner with other churches in need or begin new kingdom work in other locations. The effort to multiply creates a fostering movement that is cyclical and scalable.

APPENDIX C

Practical Suggestions for Phase III: Go to Work

Restore the Building

1. Apply a new coat of paint to both interior and exterior areas of concern.
2. Declutter the building by removing outdated, broken, and unused objects.
3. Decorate the building in a way that is warm and inviting to outsiders.
4. Install new interior and exterior lighting for practical functions, design, and safety.
5. Provide new directional signage that identifies key locations and ministry areas.
6. Refresh the landscaping and curb appeal.

Refresh the Pastor

1. Allow time off for a vacation.
2. Provide ministry assistance with visitations and outreach events.
3. Provide a preaching schedule or preaching team for added relief.

4. Encourage the congregation to give the pastor (and his family) gifts.

5. Train deacons to assist in member care.

6. Make meals and/or take a favorite dessert to the pastor.

7. Pay for additional books or resources to be added to his personal library.

8. Encourage the pastor to seek medical attention or counseling as needed.

9. Make a personal financial contribution to bless the pastor and his family.

Refocus the Congregation

1. Encourage the congregation to participate in regular and ongoing prayer.

2. Conduct revival services or a dedicated preaching series on returning to God.

3. The pastoral team should lovingly call the church to repent.

4. Provide a revitalization themed bible study such as a study of Nehemiah or the Seven Churches of Revelation.

5. Help the church to recommit themselves to worship, fellowship, discipleship, evangelism, and ministry.

Reengage the Community

1. Host a block party or cookout for the surrounding community.

2. Canvas the community with a needs assessment or survey.

3. Adopt a local school.

4. Meet poverty related needs.

5. Provide medical and dental services for free.

6. Begin an after-school tutoring program for children.

APPENDIX D

Evaluation Tools

Pastoral Evaluation Tool

Get to know the pastor personally:
- Ask about his experiences in life and ministry.
- Ask about his family.
- Ask about his own spiritual health and practices.
- Ask about his views regarding Scripture, salvation, and his philosophy of ministry.

As the pastor responds, can you discern the following elements:
- Is he called to ministry?
- Is he in the right location for his calling?
- Is he biblically and theologically sound?
- What are his strengths? Weaknesses?
- Is he committed to faithfully teaching and preaching God's Word?
- Is he passionate about evangelism?
- Is he a committed disciple maker?
- Is he the right man to lead the church in the next season of growth and renewal?

Church Evaluation Tool

Get to know more about the church:

- Ask about the status of the church and existing ministries.
- Ask about worship attendance, Sunday school participation, and financial health.
- Ask about the history of the church.
- Ask about their goals for the future.

As the pastor or key leaders respond, can you discern the following elements:

- Can we partner well with the pastor and/or key leaders?
- Are the church and/or key leaders committed to proclaiming the Gospel?
- Has the church experienced major decline in recent years? If so, what contributed to the change?
- Are the church and/or key leaders willing to accept the necessary changes?
- Are the church and/or key leaders willing to abandon their own pursuits in favor of God's preferred future for their church?

APPENDIX E:

Church Fostering Exit Interview Guide

Listen to the key leader and record all responses during exit interviews. Interview responses and learning from their perspective can help shape future fostering relationships:

- Ask about their role within the church fostering relationship.
- Ask about their overall view of the experience.
- Ask about their most memorable moments from the experience.
- Ask about their view of strengths and weaknesses from the fostering relationship.
- Ask them what they would do the same or different if given the opportunity again.
- Ask for general suggestions and recommendations that might be helpful before pursuing future fostering relationships.

As the key leader responds, discern the following elements:

- Does the key leader have a positive or negative view of church fostering?
- Did they serve in the right area of ministry according to their own strengths and giftedness?
- Should they serve again on future fostering assignments? If yes, where can they best serve churches in need? If no, why not?
- How can we apply their church fostering suggestions to improve the overall experience moving forward?

⌃⌐
END NOTES

1 Jay Strother, interview by author, Brentwood, November 29, 2023.

2 David Jackson, interview by author, January 24, 2024.

3 North American Mission Board, Manual for Church Fostering, 11.

4 Jim Bo Stewart, interview by author, December 11, 2023.

5 Ibid.

6 Ibid.

7 Jim Bo Stewart, interview by author, December 11, 2023.

8 Ephesians 5:25, 1 Thessalonians 4:16-17, Ephesians 4:11.

9 All Scripture references are in the English Standard Version (ESV) unless noted otherwise.

10 Mike Glenn, interview by author, January 03, 2024.

11 For more information, check out Thom Rainer's partnership and fostering articles on churchanswers.com or read Pathways to Partnership by Mark Hallock and Bob Bickford. Remember, relationships are complex, messy, and take time to develop.

12 Jim Bo Stewart, interview by author, December 11, 2023.

13 Ibid.

14 Mark Clifton, interview by author, December 11, 2023.

15 Mark Clifton, interview by author, December 11, 2023.

16 Ibid.

17 Jay Strother interview by author, November 29, 2023.

18 Fady Al-Hagal interview by author, January 09, 2024.

19 Church fostering is not limited to these four areas but addressing them should be part of the upfront evaluation and subsequent work. A myriad of projects can emerge as the relationship is developed, but beginning with these four general areas is recommended.

20 Church leaders should consider sharing a weekly bible study, sermon series, or brief devotional from the book of Nehemiah. Nehemiah's story of rebuilding the wall is inspiring, encouraging, and suitable for the work being accomplished in the CNF.

21 As a study of Nehemiah was suggested for addressing the physical condition of the campus, a study of the seven churches of Revelation

is recommended for dealing with the spiritual condition of the congregation. Revelation 1-3 calls church leaders to see themselves as the Lord sees them, to confess sin, and remember previous heights of health and ministry that no longer exist.

22 Mark Clifton, interview by author, December 11, 2023

23 Steven Wald, interview by author, January 09, 2024.

24 Mike Glenn, interview by author, January 03, 2024.

25 Fady Al-Hagal interview by author, January 09, 2024.

26 Mike Glenn, interview by author, January 03, 2024.

27 See Appendix C for practical suggestions to address these four areas of ministry concern.

28 The final review and evaluation experience will vary by context. Evaluation tools are readily available online with many fostering churches creating their own questions, guidelines, and rubric for grading the experience.

29 Mike Glenn, interview by author, January 03, 2024.